Charles W Greene

A Sketch of Kingston and Its Surroundings

the mining center of the famous Percha district, New Mexico

.

Charles W Greene

A Sketch of Kingston and Its Surroundings
the mining center of the famous Percha district, New Mexico

ISBN/EAN: 9783337096717

Printed in Europe, USA, Canada, Australia, Japan

Cover: Foto ©Andreas Hilbeck / pixelio.de

More available books at **www.hansebooks.com**

A SKETCH OF

KINGSTON

— AND —

ITS SURROUNDINGS

—·⊱ ⊰·—

The Mining Center of the
FAMOUS PERCHA DISTRICT,
New Mexico.

—·⊱ ⊰·—

Its Resources and Advantages Truthfully Presented to the Attention of Business
Men and Capitalists.

— · ◦ · —

—Edited by CHAS. W. GREENE.—

— · ◦ · —

Kingston, New Mexico.
Published by the Tribune Office.
1883.

WILL BE SENT ON APPLICATION

This publication is made for the purpose of presenting a reliable description of Kingston and the surrounding mining district. It will be sent to any address upon receipt of a three cent stamp to cover postage.

Address THE PUBLISHERS.

KINGSTON,

THE GEM OF THE RANGE.

———————

Few places have ever attracted so much attention within so brief a period of time as has the one which it is the purpose of this pamphlet to describe.

In a section of the country comparatively little known to the general public, but recently the exclusive home of the Indian, a locality having few attractions for the average newspaper reporter, its almost marvelous wealth of mineral deposits had never been suspected. The Kingston or Percha district is not, however, a placer district as is the region around Hillsboro, twelve miles distant. Here the precious metals are found only in lodes or veins, and the extraction of them, although extremely profitable, is a work of time, labor and patience, requiring ample resources of working capital. It is not a poor man's district, and the prospector who discovers never so good a property must wait until the attention of the capitalist has been secured before he can realize any portion of its actual value.

Such attention has been and is being attracted, and no week now passes that there are not only one but several transfers of property to men having means to develop it. To assist such parties in making their selections intelligently; to give a general idea of the location of the Percha district, relatively to the surrounding country; to present the special features of its geological formations and mineral deposits, and the extent of their development; to describe briefly the mines and prospects upon which work has been done already, and the indications presented in each, making of it so far as possible a record of the dates of location and present ownership; these are some of the objects in view in making this publication. It is not advisable to attract here the mechanic or laborer before there is work for them, or the merchant whose business is already overdone. Such industries come in their due time.

Its boundaries are not distinctly defined, but nature has so disposed the mountain ranges that it is not difficult to point out what may be fairly considered tributary to Kingston as a common center, having community interests. It is located on the eastern slope of the Black Range near its southern terminus. It includes the vallies of the chief tributaries of the Rio Percha, known as the north, middle and south Perchas, with the smaller creeks emptying into them, and the upper or western canyons or gulches drained by Trujillo creek. The Tierra Blanca district lies directly south and is disputed territory as between the Kingston and Lake Valley people, but is not likely to remain so when the toll-road recently incorporated shall be built between Kingston and Deming via the Tierra Blanca [white earth]. Over a divide to the northeast of the Hillsboro mine, on the north Percha, is the True Fissure district on a tributary of the same. Still farther north in the same direction is the Cave creek district. These are both tributary to Kingston and will become identified in interest with it.

Kingston, the mercantile center of the district, and Percha City, where are located several stores and a sawmill, are accessible by an excellent wagon road from Hillsboro, about twelve miles distant from either point. The distance is not more than eight miles, as the crow flies, almost due east from Kingston. From Hillsboro to Lake Valley it is sixteen miles, and to Nutt, the railway station, thirteen miles farther, making a total distance of forty-one miles, most of the way over roads which could hardly be improved by macadamizing. Traveling on horseback over the mountain trails the distance to Lake Valley is less than twenty miles, and to Percha City but about three miles—by the road it is six miles. By the proposed toll-road to Deming the distance will be forty-five miles. By the trail across the mountains to Georgetown it is twenty-five miles, and to Silver City, twenty-two miles farther. To the north of us, in the Range, is Chloride, forty miles, and Grafton, forty-eight miles by the trail, or fifty-five and sixty-five miles, respectively, by the wagon road via Hillsboro. From here to Socorro across the country by available routes the distance is about one hundred and sixty miles.

TOPOGRAPHY OF THE DISTRICT.

The general surface of the **district is** broken by spurs of the main range which shoot out from it in varying directions and which **are** scored by deep gulches or canyons, often presenting **almost** perpendicular walls hundreds of feet high. Standing upon the higher peaks the view is extremely picturesque, and one wonders how so **many** small mountains, or great hills, can be crowded into so small a space. As you clamber along the sides of them, even upon **a** well worn trail, you instinctively lean toward the upper side, with the consciousness that from a misstep or a fall there could be no recovery before reaching the bottom, hundreds of feet below. It requires good wind, strong limbs, steady nerves and strong boots and clothing to prospect in the mountains, or to **follow the** prospector into the out of the way places which he **ventures into in** the search for gold.

In some places the creeks have apparently cut through the solid rock which confines them to narrow channels having perpendicular walls, and into which the sun only reaches the bottom for a brief period of each day. The fall is so rapid that in the rainy season torrents come **down the** gulches of great depth and moving with tremendous force, displacing and carrying along great masses of rock, or anything, indeed, which **may** come in their way. The suddenness with which great bodies of water, falling from a "cloud-burst," sometimes come rolling down the creek beds and arroyos **is** startling, and it is not infrequent that teams or horsemen are caught and swept away in the irresistible current.

Throughout the entire district **the vallies and** mountain slopes are quite thickly covered with cedar, pine, pinon, juniper, mountain **live** oak, wild cherry, willow, birch and black walnut, all of it except the **pine** and birch of stunted growth. Several varieties of the cactus and of the soap weed, as well as the vicious Spanish bayonet, are found in abundance, and many of them will be eventually utilized for their fine, strong fibres and other properties. None of this class of plants are adapted for sitting upon and they are always ready to **repel advances toward a close** acquaintance. Occasionally the mesquit is found and other shrubs, all having a sturdy growth in keeping with the rugged surroundings. On both the north and south Perchas saw mills have been erected and considerable quantities of excellent lumber and shingles have been made from the pines, which grow to quite large size. Above Kingston, on the middle Percha, and in the less accessible ravines, to which roads are not easily constructed, there is considerable excellent timber yet undisturbed.

CLIMATIC AND OTHER ADVANTAGES.

Though situated at an altitude corresponding with that of Santa Fe—Kingston is a little higher, or about 7,400 feet—it is so much farther south that the temperature is even more agreeable than there. While the rays of the sun from June to August may be oppressive to those directly exposed to them, the least shade affords full protection, and the nights are so cool that one must sleep under cover always. In winter the thermometer rarely ever makes a record so low as zero, and it is only in the deep gorges of the highest mountains, where the sun cannot penetrate, that ice can ever be obtained. There it is only possible by flowing over and freezing a thin layer at a time. Upon the highest peaks of the main range snow lies nearly all the winter—from December to March—but never to a considerable depth. In all the mountains of this mining district it seldom remains forty-eight hours after it has fallen, and never exceeds a few inches in depth. There is not a day during the year that the miner is prevented from working by the severity of the weather, either in heat or cold. During ten months of the year it is almost continuous sunshine, the rain or snow falling, if at all, at night and always in limited quantities. The rainy season, from the middle of June to August, is but a succession of heavier showers, falling sometimes in torrents but not lasting more than an hour or two. It is not a disagreeable season in any respect as affecting personal comfort. It is warm and one would be quite willing to take a wetting except for its effect upon the clothing. There are no cold storms. It rains in right good earnest for an hour or two and then the sun shines out brighter than before.

The Percha district is more than usually fortunate in having a permanent and abundant water supply, and generally distributed. It is as pure as possible and will be ample in quantity for manufacturing purposes as well as for domestic use. There is flowing water in each of the principal branches of the Percha and in their larger tributaries throughout the entire year, and springs abound upon the mountain sides as well as in the vallies.

As a health resort this locality ought to become exceedingly popular. The uniformity of its temperature, the low degree of humidity, the purity of air and water, and the absence of any malarial or **other** injurious influences, combined with the attractions of the picturesque mountain scenery, are enough to induce a visitation from **those** who are unfortunately invalids.

There are two quite strong sulphur springs near Kingston but **the writer** is not advised that any analysis has ever been made to determine their medicinal properties.

KINGSTON, THE MERCANTILE CENTER.

It is a history of a few months only which **can be** recorded of Kingston at the present writing ; but they are months full of incident, **of** a remarkable growth, of steady advancement, of persistent effort on the part of all its people, of success in its undertakings. Within them the foundations have been laid broad and deep upon which to build a mining metropolis that shall surpass any other in the Territory.

It had not been heard of one year ago, and it was not until the Lake Valley exhibit at Denver had excited general attention and started a great stream of emigration to Southern New Mexico that the mineral wealth which surrounds it begun to be generally known and the town of Kingston became **an** established fact. It is true that many mining locations had been made within the district, and that considerable work had **been** done upon the Iron King—from which the town takes its name—showing up immense bodies of ore.

The Bullion had upon its dump a few tons of ore which when sampled surprised even its owners by **its** remarkably high grade. The Grey Eagle, with its extensive croppings had been located and **was already** involved in litigation. The value of the Superior pro**perty was** suspected and shrewd operators were negotiating for its purchase ; and there was enough in a general way to attract the overflow of miners, merchants and camp followers which Lake Valley could not make room for.

About the same time came information that "float" had been **found** upon the Solitaire, **three** miles from Kingston, on the North

Percha, which was practically solid mineral (sulphide, yielding eighty per cent. of fine silver). Not only was it in little nuggets, it was in masses, one of them weighing three hundred and forty pounds. The property was bonded by Tabor & Wurtzebach for $100,000, and a cash payment of $10,000 was made upon it. The large piece of float referred to was taken to the Denver Exposition where it shared the honors with the six hundred and forty pound piece of chloride from Lake Valley.

The press of the whole country became actively interested and the name and fame of the camp was circulated far and wide. As a result of all these influences people came pouring in till not less, probably, than three thousand had come to view the "promised land."

Kingston grew as by magic. Lots upon its main street advanced on the run from nothing to a thousand dollars each. Purchasers could be found for lots in the several additions and the question of title was hardly considered for a moment. Lumber and building materials could not be gotten fast enough; mechanics could command their own price. The road from the railroad was alive with vehicles of every description, stages, hacks, freight wagons and family wagons. Even the patient burro plodded along, doing his share to fill up the country.

But there was too much of a good thing all at once. Prospectors found less than a claim apiece for all who came, and the choice of them taken long before their arrival. Miners and laborers were too many for the demand. Of merchants there was quite too large a proportion.

The flurry of excitement was soon over. While no one could gainsay that the mines were as good as represented, every one could appreciate that it would take time, patience, perseverance and capital to develop them. The floating element drifted away; business settled into legitimate channels. Those who determined to stay curtailed expenses, and adopted the methods of established communities. The delay in obtaining materials was a fortunate hindrance, preventing the construction of too many buildings, so that there are few more than the actual need.

A more beautiful town-site could hardly be selected. It occupies a plateau in a cove of the mountains, elevated a little above the Middle Percha, the waters of which course through the town lengthwise and parallel with its main street. **It** furnishes an abundant supply of water for every purpose. The principal street is eighty feet wide, extending through the town as originally laid out, and also through the upper and lower additions. There is a gradual descent toward the east, and there is quite sufficient space immediately **adjacent** for a population of twenty thousand.

The first survey on the townsite was commenced August 21st by Parker **&** Taylor, and was of the Home Ticket mining claim, owned by **A.** Barnaby. Next was the Lula claim, belonging to Fraser & Holt, and then the **Grand View** mill-site, below Water street, owned by Pressly Johnson. The Copper Queen claim, adjoining the Home Ticket, was also platted, and later the Hornet, across the creek, **was** put on the market by Barnaby and Webster, and a **number of** residence lots were sold from it.

Meantime the Iron King mill-site, above the town, was purchased by Messrs. Boss, Ritchie and others and a company was organized. The site was surveyed and platted and some sales made, but there has been as yet but little building upon it. As a residence locality it cannot be excelled; it offers some of the prettiest building sites to be found anywhere.

The Kingston Town Company was organized October 1st, 1882, by T. F. Chapman, James A. Lockhart, Robert Hopper, Col. J. C. Logan, Frank Adams, C. H. Phelps, Thomas Kelly, Ellis Miller, **H. G. Clark** and J. C. Roberts. The property purchased constitutes **the** eastern portion of the **town** and includes the Galveston, Old Iowa, Eureka, Mexican Central, Kentucky, Last Chance, and **other** mill-site locations. To put **the** property in form, fractions were purchased from surrounding mining claims, the whole making about five hundred lots, 25 by 100 feet being the standard size. The first officers of the company were T. **F.** Chapman, president; G. W. Hartmann, secretary; J. A. Lockhart, treasurer, and Messrs. Chapman, Lockhart, Miller, Roberts and Hopper, directors. About one hundred **dred lots** have **been sold.** Several proprietary interests have changed hands so that the present owners are Messrs. Chapman, Lockhart, Hopper, Maxwell and Clark, and W. W. Maxwell is the present secretary. Extensive improvements are in progress; the streets are **being** cleared and fencing the blocks is being done under contract. The location is a very desirable one and covers the water privileges and sites where the mills, smelters and other manufactories of the district will necessarily be located—some of them in the near future. Its surface is enough diversified to insure good drainage and furnishes desirable business and residence locations.

At the present time nearly all of the business is located upon the main street and nearly all of the mercantile and mechanical industries are well represented. The Percha Bank was established several months since, and the TRIBUNE newspaper and job office, in which this pamphlet is printed and bound, has been well supported since the first of the year.

Its society is characteristic of the frontier, but contains a greater number of refined and educated people than one would expect to find so far from the comforts and conveniences to which they have been accustomed in eastern homes. The love of adventure or the desire for gain has brought the head of the family, and the wife and children come that they may be near and share with him the privations and toil which fall to his lot. As rapidly as possible they gather about them the luxuries as well as the necessities of life; they improve and beautify their homes, and when they have struck it rich live as opulently as the most prosperous capitalists of the older states. The rough board house is often furnished in far better style than its exterior betokens, and probably there is as much real enjoyment and family contentment amid such surroundings as in the brown stone or marble palaces of the great cities.

Private schools have been well supported almost from the first, although the number of children is proportionately much smaller than in an agricultural district. Steps have been taken to secure the organization of a school district, and until such time as the public funds are available good schools will be sustained by personal subscription.

As to churches, this has not seemed to be a specially inviting field for missionaries. No church buildings have been erected, nor have any societies been organized.

Good public order has always been maintained. Life and property is more secure than in many older communities, and though there is no local government except as represented in a justice of the peace and a deputy sheriff there are but few infractions of the law, and those of a trivial character. There is as much business honor and as few bad debts as will be found anywhere. Although it is by no means unpopular to take a drink of beer or whiskey, and temperance societies would not secure a large membership in the camp, there is but little drinking to excess, and no more drunkenness on the streets than is usual elsewhere.

PERCHA CITY.

The finding of the rich float on the Solitaire and the general prospects of the North Percha neighborhood, was the occasion, in the latter part of August, of locating a trading point there, and it was followed by the laying off of a townsite. The location is well chosen at a point where the valley of Carbonate creek—furnishing the town an abundant supply of water—widens, giving ample room for a large population. J. W. McCuistion was the first merchant, coming from Chloride. No road had yet been built nor trade of any kind established, though the surrounding country was full of prospectors to the number of several hundred. He packed his stock in trade over the mountains. It consisted of three hundred cigars, five gallons of whisky, six bottles of champagne, eighteen bottles of beer, and $8.75 in cash for a working capital. His success is evidenced by a large log store-room, which cost him $300, and a stock of goods in house and cellar which has cost him $3,000. He has also secured mines and interests in mines which promise a yet larger return.

The townsite was located August 28th, by John Bachus and — McDonald. The construction of the wagon road to a connection with the Hillsboro and Kingston road was commenced September 5th and the first wagon came into camp on the 12th. The town was surveyed on the 15th and was platted on a box cover. Of three hundred lots, each 25 by 140 feet, one hundred and twenty have been sold for from fifteen to forty dollars each. For a time business was lively, but there was a serious disadvantage in having no stage line. The population reached at one time as many as five hundred.

A. D. Osborne was the second merchant, also coming from Chloride, opening the Ore saloon and dealing principally in wet groceries. John Graden came from El Paso and started a restaurant. J. T. Nickerson came with a restaurant and boarding house. Ballou & Cook opened another saloon, now closed. Mike Mason started in the same business, also gone. Mr. Carmichael opened a small store; he has also departed. Later J. C. Roberts opened a meat market and then William Bratten came in with a livery stable and Samuel Nelson is the camp shoemaker. A postoffice was established several months since with J. W. McCuistion as postmaster.

During the fall a saw mill was erected just above the town by W. E. Pratt & Co., with T. E. Harrington in charge. It is a well appointed mill and they have already manufactured a large quantity of lumber and shingles and have kept in operation all winter. It has supplied a large share of the demand for building and mine lumber at Kingston and in the district generally since it went into operation.

There are many good prospects on every side of the town and as the mines become developed and are put in full operation it must become a point of considerable importance.

THE PERCHA MINING DISTRICT.

The mining interest of the district is the paramount one to all others; it is the foundation upon which all other industries must rest. It is, of course, in its infancy and its full development will require time and a large expenditure of capital. The resources of the camp are but comparatively little known, a shaft one hundred feet deep being the rare exception, while there is not one in the district two hundred feet deep at the present writing—March 20th.

An article written a few weeks since for the San Francisco EXAMINER by Mr W. F. Hogan contains a very careful description of the general features of the camp and of its geological formations, from which the liberty is taken to make some extracts.

"The formation consists chiefly of a dolomitic limestone, occurring in regular strata, dipping slightly to the south of east and having a general northerly and southerly strike. This limestone is cut through in many places by dykes of intrusive porphyry and cross courses of quartz. The porphyry has a general course nearly parallel with the limestone, while the quartz ledges run in a general northeasterly and southwesterly direction, cutting through both the porphyry and limestone in their course. These porphyry dykes and quartz ledges sometimes assume large proportions so far as width goes, and in the case of the former not only are they exceptional in width but in length also, one in particular—apparently the chief one in the district—being plainly traceable for miles. In some places the porphyry fails to intrude itself clear through the limestone to the surface, but after rising to a certain plane, has spread out and is now found in the condition of an interstratification in the sedimentary rocks. This is accounted for on the hypothesis that only at the weaker places of the original formation, was the intrusive force sufficient to cause the limestone to break and allow the molten lava access to the top. Hence it is that at points along their course the porphyry dykes are apparently lost, and also that the lime sometimes appears overlying the porphyry, as shown by development shafts and erosion in the adjacent gulches. Argillaceous limestone is also found in portions of the district, and always overlying the dolomite. It does not, however, appear to have exercised any influence in the deposition of the contents of the mineral waters in their flow, although ore is sometimes found between it and the underlying strata. It is to the presence of these dykes, and the numerous faults, slides and fractures in the limestone, caused by them, that the Percha district owes its mineral wealth. The quartz ledges which mark the surface of the country are also noted for their metalliferous value. They present no special features deserving of mention. Their origin, together with the deposition of the metallic compounds held by them, being undoubtedly contemporaneous with the formation of the ore belts and veins of the porphyritic and limestone rocks. Naturally in such a formation the experienced prospector looks for more than one distinct type of mines. In this respect the Percha country is remarkable, not only in presenting several well defined species, but also in showing the characteristics of each kind to a marked degree.. Thus it is that there are contact-fissures, limestone deposits, quartz leads and fissures in trachyte. The first are those whose main ore bodies are or will be found at the point of juncture between either edge of the dykes and the limestone through which they cut. The second are those in which the ore is found interbedded with and lying conformably to the general plane of the lime stratification. In both these classes of mines, and notably in the first mentioned, the ore is found frequently branching off from the main shoots and forming pockets irregularly distributed throughout the limestone, but occurring principally along the joint planes of the fractures and faults with which the latter rock abounds. Where two or more of these fractures meet there is usually quite a large pocket of mineral—sometimes of high grade and sometimes low. The quartz veins are of a more uniform character, apparently, as regards the occurrence of the ore contained by them. They are very prominent factors in the geological structure of the Percha district, as attested by the prominence and frequency of their outcroppings. They present no such interesting and complex features as do the others mentioned, the ore being a base mass of quartz mineralized to a greater or less degree, according as it is taken from an ore shoot, or distant from one. There is more or less mineral, however, to be found throughout nearly all of the quartz ledges, as numerous assay tests have proven. The fissure veins in the trachyte are yet an element of undetermined importance as regards the part they are to take in the future of the district. One of them thus far opened to a limited extent has proven to be of extraordinary good promise. The veins at Bodie, California, and other noted mining sections, are in trachyte, which is evidence sufficient to warrant a belief highly favorable to the discovery of many good mines in that formation as it exists here. It is a field in which little has been done and one that offers great inducements to the prospector. The best established and most accepted theory of the manner in which mineral has been deposited in the rocks, would account for its presence in the quartz, contact-fissures and the limestone, by its having been brought there through the flowing of the siliceous waters. These had their origin undoubtedly in the trachyte itself, hence it would be unreasonable to suppose the fissures naturally occurring in that rock to be destitute of metallic values. The fact that where found they carry metalliferous quartz as a vein-filling, is proof not only of the origin of the ore deposits of the Percha district but also of the statement that much may be looked for from the trachyte fissures in the future.

"The metallic compounds produced by the mines of this district are varied, as is usual with all mineral sections. The predominating form in which silver is found is a sulphide, or silver glance. This is commonly called, by the miners and prospectors, "black metal," or "malleable silver." Chloride of silver and bromide is found, with also some ruby and silver in a pure state, or native. Argentiferous galena, carbonate of lead carrying silver, together with pyritiferous copper and copper carbonates are found in some of the mines. Antimony and zinc blende, or "black jack," and iron pyrites are also found in the ores. Brown iron oxide and oxide of manganese prevail in many of the veins, the latter being particularly plentiful and forming the outcropping, or mineral blossom of a very large proportion of the mines. The gangue of the veins is usually quartz, with heavy spar, calcite and talc, intermixed often with felsite. Some veins show these minerals in different combinations, one predominating over the others, as a general thing. This latter circumstance varies with the character of the mine."

From the foregoing description of the character of the mines about Kingston, the miner and prospector can glean many things that will enable him to form an opinion as to the merits of the Percha district. It is an admitted proposition among mining men that a country whose formation is cut up by dykes and cross ledges, and greatly faulted thereby, is one, which if possessed of mineral wealth at all, is of a very superior kind. This being so—and experience has proven it—the outlook for the mines and the district of Percha, is one of the brightest to be found throughout the whole of the Rocky mountain region. The mines thus far have done splendidly, and give abundant grounds for unlimited confidence in their future, while the prospects here are invariably of the most promising kind. Capital is needed to stimulate the task of development upon the properties of men too poor to push to a successful issue, the work of prospecting the veins. Once it comes Kingston will acheive a notoriety that will be as substantial as it will be brilliant. Splendid opportunities are offered those who come with a desire to invest. Instances are frequent where prospectors are willing to give from one-quarter to one-half of their claim to have it developed to a paying basis, while whole claims, eligibly situated, and presenting indications of a positive character for the discovery of good ore can be purchased outright on the most moderate terms. No place offers superior inducements of this kind, and certainly none can better substantiate its claims to to intrinsic merit than can the Percha district. The mineral is here in large quantities and of high grade and work alone is needed to reveal it and make wealthy the owners of the mines. What has been done thus far is but an earnest of what can and will be done in the future. The attention of all is called to these things with a confidence in the belief that they are just as represented, and from an actual knowledge of the facts, circumstances and needs surrounding the district.

As it is the express purpose of this pamphlet to direct the eye of those interested towards the mines, the following pages will be devoted to brief descriptions of the leading mines and prospects located in the different camps adjacent and tributary to the town of Kingston, commencing with the

MIDDLE PERCHA.

The mines of this portion of the district were the first to attract the attention of outsiders in this direction. The first were located in 1880. Despite the early date of their location nothing more than mere prospecting work has been done, although in some instances that character of work alone not only has demonstrated the actual merits of the properties, but has also resulted in bringing large returns to the owners over and above the money spent in that direction.

The prominent mine is the Bullion, which by reason of the bulk and richness of its ore has made for itself a name that is famous throughout New Mexico. This mine was located in August, 1881, by Geo. W. Hunsaker and Arthur Phelps, who after its discovery excavated several surface openings and one shaft of about fifteen feet in depth. One of the openings on the surface was at a point where there was a large out-cropping of black oxide of iron and manganese, and this when cut into a very few feet disclosed ore that gave very high returns by assay. One of the owners, fearful that it would pinch out declined to work it further and prevailed upon his partner to offer it for sale, which was done, and in a short time it passed into the possesion of the company now owning it. This company is composed mostly of gentlemen who are conversant with the details of practical mining and who since taking possession of the property have developed and extracted the ore which has yielded them such handsome returns upon their original investment. The price paid the owners was $3,500. The amount of ore extracted to date figures up to the splendid sum of $80 000. When it is considered that the total number of linear feet of work done will not exceed 500, and that of that number over 150 feet are dead work, consisting of a cross drift entirely out of ore, but run for the better development of the mine, it will be understood that the Bullion is entitled to the great reputation it possesses. In other words there has been over $160 extracted for every foot of ground, straight measurement, excavated in the mine. Such a showing would be considered immense in any country, and it certainly speaks volumes in favor of the character and richness of the mines of this section. The Bullion is of the contact-fissure class of veins, and this, in connection with the circumstance that the ore produced thus far has come out of the limestone east of the vein proper, argues much in favor of the future excellence of this splendid property. When the contact is reached and that portion of the mine developed, there is every reason to look for a much greater showing than has ever yet been disclosed. The ore of the Bullion is of exceptionally high grade, averaging upwards of $500 per ton. It is not unusual to take out pieces weighing from fifty to three hundred pounds that will average at the rate of $1 000 to $5,000 per ton. A pocket of ore recently struck in the mine, consisted of a mass of nearly pure sulphide of silver, average specimens of which returned by assay a value of over $18,000 per ton. Several hundred pounds of this rich stuff were taken out. The ore is found in a gangue of lime spar, talc and occasionally some quartz or other siliceous matter. The mine is supplied upon the surface with an office building, boarding and sleeping houses, blacksmith shop, ore house, etc. An excellent wagon road leads from the mine down to and connecting with the road leading into Kingston, just below town. Mr. T. F. Chapman, the superintendent, is a very able and accommodating manager, and one who takes pleasure in showing the product of the mine and explaining its features to parties interested. He took hold of the property when it was a prospect, and by his faith and energy has developed a bonanza. Several offers of high prices have been made for the mine and all refused. While it is not improbable that the owners would sell if they were to be offered their own figures, they are in no hurry and it is safe to assert that the mine is not begging a purchaser. The ore shipments from the mine have all been made to the Argo works, near Denver, Colorado.

Next to the Bullion, and joining it upon the north, is the Superior, a property already known far and near as one which not only has great intrinsic merit but which also promises to do much in the way of ore shipments during the year 1883. It is situated upon the same vein as the Bullion and presents throughout the sam

general characteristics of ore and ore deposits. Considerable work
has been done upon the Superior, more in fact than upon any other
mine in the camp, except the Iron King, and certainly the resultant
effects are such as are calculated to inspire feelings of the utmost
confidence in it upon the part of **those owning** the mine as well as
convincing owners of property similarly situated, of the future value
of their claims. **The Superior mine was located in** the summer of
1881, by Frazer & Deemer, a couple of prospectors from Georgetown,
New Mexico. Ore was found in several places upon the surface of
the claim and several small openings were made at those points.
The assays obtained **were** very encouraging, running from a few
ounces into the hundreds. In the fall of 1882, and soon after the
development of the ore body in the Bullion, the Superior was purchased by a company of California capitalists, among whom were
Hearst & Head, Col. Logan, ex-Governor Perkins and others, to-
gether with Capt. Thos. **Burns, who was one of the original purchasers** of the Bullion. **Capt. Burns took immediate charge of the**
property and at once commenced active development. A shaft was
sunk in the limestone to a depth of ninety feet, and at that point a
drift was started to the west towards **the** edge of the porphyry.
Three ore bodies were cut in this drift before reaching the contact.
This where struck was found devoid of anything of value save what
was found as gangue matter, indicating clearly the presence of the
vein. Sinking was commenced, and it was but **a** short distance until a large body of low grade ore was discovered. Down through
this the work was pushed until **at a** depth of seventy feet, a body of
splendid ore was encountered, rich in both gold and silver. This
was the great strike that agitated the whole of the Percha district
and set at rest all doubts **and fears that** may heretofore been enter-
tained regarding the future **of the** camp. Several tons of the new
ore were broken and average tests of its value show it to be worth
$1 200 per ton. The extent of this ore body has not yet been **de-**
termined but enough has been done to show that **it is** of large proportions. Now that this much has been accomplished, **more may**
be looked for **in** the lower workings of the **mine. Aside from the**
development just described, there has been, as indicated in the foregoing, a considerable amount **of work** done elsewhere on the Superi-
or. Most of this has been confined **to** places where there were in-

dications of ore out in the limestone and distant from the porphyry, while at one or more places the vein has been opened along its extent. None of these but what show the presence of ore in greater or less quantity and of varying quality from high to low grade. In what is known as number seven working, a nice seam of good ore is showing, of good quality. In number four the vein has been sunk upon for seventy feet showing ore and vein matter the whole distance for a width of from two to five feet. Since the making of the rich strike work has been directed towards the excavation of an incline shaft from the surface downward, in order that the task of proper development may be facilitated in the future. An improved California whim is in use at the incline. There are other surface improvements connected with the mine consisting of an office building, residence, blacksmith shop and stable. R. B. Taylor, a gentleman of ripe mining experience is the superintendent of the Superior The mine is being developed by him in a systematic manner, and should the future warrant it there is little doubt but that the company will erect works adapted to the treatment of their own ores. The extent of the vein on the Superior is such that once it is opened up a lengthened period of prosperity is in store for the mine. The developments on the Superior have proven one thing that is of inestimable benefit to claim owners in the Percha district. This is that it matters but little whether the surface material assays high or not. The bodies of rich ore lie comparatively deep and those having the nerve and means to go down on their veins will almost undoubtedly get good ore if the surface and other indications are right to commence with. Practical experience has demonstrated that in all camps where silver is found as a sulphide that the ore is just as liable to be of very low grade on the top as it is to be the reverse. Once the proper depth is gained—and this varies in different localities—the ore will be found, if it exists in bulk at all, to be of a high grade character. And this is one of the reasons, too, which induces those of experience to put such great faith in the district.

The Caledonia lays near the Superior and is owned by George Hartman and Marshal Dansby. It was located in February, 1882. Aside from some surface digging to find the lead the chief work has deen done at two places of twelve or fifteen feet each. The croppings are oxide of iron and manganese, all of it carrying some mineral as shown by the assays, and showing more and better as depth is attained. It is in quite large quantities but the vein has not yet been found in place. A small seam of ore at the bottom of one of the openings has assayed up as high as $300 in silver per ton.

· The Comstock lying west and alongside the Caledonia is on the opposite or west side of the hill. It is opened in a contact betwen porphyry and lime, at least seven feet in width, dipping into the hill. Where opened the crevice is filled with iron and manganese. From a seam next the porphyry wall at a depth of sixteen feet ore was taken which gave an assay value of $625.40, and assays from the croppings have returned from five to forty-one ounces. The vein is the same which shows in the Black Colt and crops out its full width on the surface over one hundred feet from the shaft where it is now opened. The Comstock is owned by James Dawson Joshua Roberts and others and was located March 30, 1880. It gives excellent promise of developing into a mine.

The Lady Franklin belongs to Dan Dugan and John Donohoe. It was located in 1881. It lies west of the Superior and south of the Caledonia. The vein pitches at an angle of forty-five degrees, or a little more than the slope of the hillside. Its pitch corresponds with that of the Comstock on the other side of the hill, and is in a contrary direction to that of the Caledonia. The vein matter corresponds with that in adjoining claims, with a mixture of talc and felsite. It has given good assays all the way down, being now at a depth of about thirty feet.

The Mountain Chief is owned by Ed. Doheny, Thomas Grady, Tim Corcoran and James Delaney. It was located in November, 1880. It is located diagonally across a ridge of porphyry and limestone. On top of the hill a shaft has been sunk on the contact, nearly vertical, in a mass of disintegrated iron-stained porphyry. There is a wide belt on the surface covered by iron boulders, apparently float, but the source has not yet been discovered. Down in the gulch an iron capping covers a vein of quartz and spar, with iron and copper pyrites. The vein is well defined, nearly vertical, with lime walls. The ore that has been taken out assays well, some of it averaging fifty dollars. The vein is only opened to a depth of twelve feet.

The Polar Star is the north extension of the Superior mine and covers a tract of ground that shows abundant surface indications of mineral. It has been worked upon at several places, the principal openings being close to the south end line and near to the Superior ground. Two shafts sunk there have produced very good ore, the average in ton lots running upwards of $200, and picked specimens going very much higher. The ore so far taken out came from the limestone and is of a quartzose character. It shows native silver and chloride throughout. At another portion of the claim an opening has been made upon a surface showing or outcropping of iron and manganese, carrying silver. The Polar Star is regarded as one of the leading claims of this district and rightly so. It is owned by Col. Logan and Geo. Hunsaker, the latter in connection with Arthur Phelps, being the locator of the property. A shipment of about two tons of first-class ore has been made.

The Silver Queen, located in April, 1882, by Burke and Skipp, is along the course of an immense contact-fissure vein between limestone and porphyry. It is opened in several places on the vein and everywhere shows indications of great strength and permanance. The center workings, which are the most prominent, are confined to the middle of the width of the vein and are all in vein matter, top, sides and bottom. The vein at this point has a width of eighty feet by actual measurement, and wherever stripped or penetrated shows the same character of filling. These center workings consist of an adit level, run in thirty feet, to a point where it branches off, the main branch continuing on for a distance of forty feet further. The second branch goes beyond the parting place only a few feet, and at the face a shaft is down to about twenty feet. Every foot of these workings is in vein matter all more or less mineralized, and carrying pieces of ore from which high assays have been obtained. This vein stuff consists principally of decomposed iron stained porphyry, brown iron and manganese. Assays have been obtained from the material described, running $4.00, $12.00, $104 and $117 respectively. A general sample of the disintegrated vein matter returned $12.00 per ton. With so large and strong a vein, so well filled with mineralized matter there is every reason to look for much from the future of this property. Doubtless the surface ore has undergone a leaching out process at the hands of nature, it being of a free character.

and so easily acted upon that the course of the vein is traceable by a marked depression in the hill through which it passes. Naturally the apex ore of a large vein of this description, is found debased through the influence of surface infiltration. It is the candid opinion of some of the best judges of mines in New Mexico that the Silver Queen will prove an immense mine upon deep development. This is an opinion in which the writer of this pamphlet shares. The course of the vein is north and south.

Silver Queen, Number 1, is located parallel with and adjoins the Silver Queen upon the west. The ore is of a quartz character, carrying galena, sulphide of silver, chloride and native silver. There are two openings on the claim, consisting of a shaft eighteen feet deep, and an adit level eighteen feet in length. As yet the ore is low grade, the assays showing only the presence of a small amount of silver. Burke and Skipp are the owners and locators of the claim.

Silver Queen, Number 2, is an east and west location, its east end line joining with the west side line of the Silver Queen, Number 1. It shows a vein of iron sulphurets in porphyry, and was located more with a view to taking up and protecting the water right of that portion of Sawpit canon, in which it is situated, than for any other purpose. Burke and Skipp are the owners and locators.

The Black Colt is a property upon which considerable surface work has been done. At numerous points on the claim there are outcroppings of iron and manganese, nearly all of which have silver in greater or less quantity. Several of these have been stripped off, and three shafts have been sunk. The vein is a contact-fissure, between limestone and porphyry. One shaft is down a depth of forty-five feet, one over sixty feet and one twenty-five feet, all showing an abundance of mineralized vein matter. Assays from ore taken out have returned from fifty to sixty dollars per ton. Peterson and Simpson located and own the claim.

The Savage is located alongside the Superior mine, and is owned by Frazer, Holt and Cosgrove. It covers quite an extent of the same belt of limestone as do the Bullion and Superior mines and has also within its lines a contact-fissure. The owners have put down a fifty foot shaft on an iron capping in the limestone. No work of consequence has yet been done on the contact. Some very favorable assays have been obtained from ore out of the Savage.

The Little Jimmie is owned by Moore, Bennett & Co. It is opened in two places from the surface by means of shafts sunk in limestone. Quite a large body of low grade ore has been struck in one of the shafts and development is being done with a view to reaching a better grade of ore. In character the ore is similar to that produced by the Bullion and Superior, but the value so far is as stated, low. The workings of the Little Jimmie are in the same lime belt as are the two famous mines mentioned.

The Southwick is east of the Savage and parallel with it. It is owned by Burke and O'Rourke. A ten foot shaft shows vein matter consisting of iron and manganese.

The Evening Star, west of and parallel with the Bullion and Superior, is owned by Burke and Skipp. It shows a contact on the surface.

The Silver Bullion, owned by Burke and Skipp, lies close to the Bullion upon the east. It has a shaft sunk on a contact, and makes a fair showing of mineralized vein matter

The Uncle Jack is owned by Dugan, Donohoe and McNally. It is on a contact between lime and porphyry, and is opened by a shaft to the depth of eighty feet. The vein matter is iron and manganese, all mineralized, but of low grade.

The Empire is the extension upon the north, of the Iron King, and is owned by Dan Dugan. It is in the same lime belt as the Iron King and shows upon the surface the same iron cropping. There are about fifty feet of work done upon the claim and some assays have been obtained that show well. Average samples of the ore assay from twenty-two to sixty odd ounces.

The Palmetto is owned by Skipp, Burke and Barnaby. It lies parallel with the Iron King and Empire. No work of consequence has been done upon it, but there is the same surface showing of iron and manganese, as is to be found upon the surface of claims in that locality.

The Judge is owned by Skipp, Burke and Thompson. It has a shaft upon it twelve feet deep, in iron and manganese, from which some fair assays in silver have been obtained.

The John Brant is owned by Dawson, Ferguson, and Roach. It is opened by a twelve foot shaft showing excellent indications of the same character as that exhibited in other claims of the neighborhood.

The Iron Mask is owned by O'Donnell and Stanley. It is the north extension of the Silver Queen and shows an extensive outcrop of the same material as that held between the walls of the "Queen." It is opened by two shafts, one twenty feet deep and one ten feet deep. The vein matter assays from twelve to fifteen dollars in silver.

The Roman Beauty is owned by Timothy Kelly and Thos. Donnor. Shows the same croppings as the Iron Mask and is opened by means of a twenty foot shaft. Some high assays have been obtained from ore out of this claim, one going as high as $1,400.

The Star of the West is owned by Skipp, Burke, O'Donnell and Barnaby. No work of consequence has been done upon it but there is a good surface show of iron and manganese.

The Nip and Tuck is a fractional claim lying between the Iron King, Miner's Dream and the Mountain Chief. It is finely located, lying in the midst of a group of excellent claims. It is located along the course of a porphyry and lime contact, and shows iron and manganese cropping. The owners are Burke, Delaney and Corcoran.

The Moore Bros. and Co., have several claims north and east of the Bullion and Superior. They are located with good discernment as regards the probable existence of ore. One of these, the Fijiean, shows a strong outcrop of ferrugineous quartz. The decomposition of the iron has completely metamorphosed whole portions of the original rock, until it resembles what is commonly called "burnt iron." This claim has produced ore from a ten foot shaft that gives encouraging returns in silver when tested by assay.

The foregoing embraces most of the mines and prospects which are of a uniform character, lying north and east of the Iron King and Miner's Dream, and south of those which would come properly under the head of North Percha mines. They are grouped as given for the sake of convenience in the compilation of this pamphlet.

The mines, commencing with the Iron King and Miner's Dream, which lie south and west of the ones already described, will now be taken up, embracing all those of prominence and prospective value situated upon the east and west slopes of Kentuck mountain, the adjacent mountain upon which the Black Eyed Susan, Andy Johnson and Brush Heap are located, and all others about which it has been possible to gather information, and which properly belong under the head of Middle Percha mines.

The Iron King is perhaps the best and most widely known of all the properties in the Percha district. **It was** the first location, and by reason of its quick sale at handsome figures, and the subsequent development of its vast ore bodies, it caused to be fixed upon this section the attention of prospectors and mining men from all **sections** of the country. The mine was located in November, 1880, by **Elliott** and Forbes, who sold the property when there **was only an** eight foot shaft upon it, for the sum of $25,000, Philadelphia **people being the** purchasers. It is located upon a zone or belt of limestone in which the ore is mostly found lying conformably with **the plane** of the strata of the enclosing rock, and belongs to that class which comes under the head of limestone deposits. **It is, in fact**, the chief representative of that class of mines. It differs **locally** from most of the others because the strata of limestone which originally covered the ore along the east half of the claim's length has been almost entirely scored off, leaving exposed, close to the surface, the ore of the the vein, except where covered by thin scales of limestone, or the detritus incident to all mountain surfaces. The middle workings of the mine comprise two shafts and an adit level. One of these shafts —the main one of the mine—is down seventy feet and shows ore all the way, at the sides and bottom. The first forty feet is ore that averages well in lead, being a decomposed quartz, carrying lead car-**bonates and** iron. The balance continues in ore of a slightly different description, consisting of **brown** oxide of iron principally, carrying copper carbonates and showing bunches of galena distributed throughout the **mass**. Three hundred feet **west,** or near the center of the claim, a shaft is down through limestone eighty odd feet, fol-**lowing a streak of ore** bearing lead carbonates. Between the two shafts an adit level is in forty feet, showing ore the whole way, top, **sides and bottom. It** is of the same general character, being a brown and red oxide of iron, galena and lead carbonate. Near the north end there are two shafts of fifty feet each, in black iron and manganese, carrying some lead. For two hundred and forty feet, the distance between these two shafts, an open cut has been excavated to a depth of ten feet, showing ore all the way. At the extreme north end and close to the center end stake, there is a quartz cross course which has been stripped along its length for forty feet, producing considerable galena ore. At the south end there is a twenty-five foot shaft in iron and manganese ore. The ore from this shaft averages sixty-five ounces in silver. At the extreme south end there is a cut of sixty-five feet, in black iron, and from the bottom of this an incline shaft is down forty-six feet all in ore of the same character of iron and manganese, averaging fairly in lead. Fifty feet east of this is another cut twenty-five feet long, with a vertical shaft forty feet deep. From this it will be seen that the territory of the Iron King, embraces an extensive tract of valuable mineral bearing ground. Exploitation shows that the ore exists at every point beneath the surface of at least one-half the property, and extremely strong probabilities for its continuing under most of the remaining surface. It also shows that this body of ore is over seventy feet thick, which of itself is something enormous. While it is not what would be called high grade, the ore is sufficiently valuable to furnish good returns over the cost of mining, handling and treating, when once the district is supplied with local smelting establishments. The ore ranges from twenty to ninety ounces in silver and from twelve to sixty per cent. in lead. The property is now owned by a private corporation of ample means and first-class financial standing, and is being developed with a view to demonstrating its actual worth, and also for the purpose of extracting and marketing the great quantities of ore known to exist in it. E. Lucien Richie is the resident agent and general manager at Kingston, and Wm. Welch is the working superintendent at the mine.

The Miner's Dream lies east of and immediately parallel with the Iron King. It is owned by Delaney, Corcoran and company. The ore so far found lies in an interstratafied condition in the limestone, but the general trend of it is toward a contact-fissure which is plainly indicated upon the surface of the ground covered by the property. The main development is an adit level which has followed ore from the surface and which shows a fine body of ore several feet in thickness, at the breast. It is an argentiferous galena, selected samples of which return high assay values. Considerable blue and green carbonate of copper has been produced from this mine. There is a large dump of ore at the entrance of the main opening.

The Pinafore is located south of the Iron King and Miner's

Dream. It is owned by Burke & Skipp. Shows surface indications and is the same character of mine as the "King." It has a shaft down fifty-four feet and has produced ore which assays well in silver.

The Cave mine, owned by Dugan and Donohoe, is in the same locality. It has a shaft twenty feet deep, with good ore of a quartz character, from some of which high assays have been obtained.

The Ready Cash is a contact-fissure, upon which the work done has resulted in making a very handsome looking prospect. There is a well defined streak of lead carbonate ore, and the silver value is highly encouraging, running upwards of one hundred ounces. This is one of the best undeveloped claims on the Middle Percha.

The Kentuck is owned by Bledsoe, Kelly, Roberts and company. It is opened in several places and makes a good show of valuable ore in considerable quantity.

The Frazer is owned by Frazer and Holt. Has a shaft twenty feet deep, showing ore carrying silver. Assays of over $200 have been obtained from ore out of this property. The vein is from three to four feet wide.

The Andy Johnson, Black Eyed Susan and Brush Heap mines comprise a group that were located and are now owned by Forbes and Elliott, the two pioneer prospectors of the district. The discovery of these two claims was the cause of the first excitement ever experienced by the Percha district, as from ore found in them very high assays were obtained. They were discovered soon after the Iron King and are of the same character of mines as the "King," viz., interstratified or bedded deposits in limestone, the overlying strata being an argyllaceous limestone, or lime shale. The most important mine of the group, because of the superior amount of development done upon it, is the Andy Johnson. It has been opened on the vein by a shaft 115 feet deep and two levels run on the vein, one at thirty feet from the surface and one from the bottom of the shaft. The ore throughout will average thirty inches in thickness and ranges in value from $10 to $1,000 per ton. No general average of the vein was ever taken, but assorted lots mill upwards of $100 per ton. There is a large dump of ore at the mine which came out of the workings and an average sample of that returned at the rate of $75.00 per ton. The Andy Johnson was the first mine in the district give a high assay return, a piece off the outcrop going $750.

The Black Eyed Susan is in the same mineral belt and is opened by an adit twenty-five feet in length, showing ore from two to three feet wide the whole distance. It averages $50.00 in silver and from thirty to forty per cent. in lead.

The Brush Heap is also on the same lime belt. It is opened in several places on the surface, the principal work being an open cut, six by ten feet. The vein here is fully six feet wide and filled with ore from wall to wall. Some very high assays have been had from ore out of this mine, but the general average, as determined by actual tests made by disinterested parties, is $61.00 in silver.

The Eclipse is parallel with the Black Eyed Susan, and is owned by Daniel Dugan. It has a surface opening showing it to be of the same character. The ore assays well.

The Illinois mine lies south of those just described, and is the same character of mine, both as regards its manner of occurrence and character of ore. It is owned by Colonel Logan, A. W. Harris, D. H. Jackson, J. W. Southwick and others. The main opening is an adit in about thirty feet, following a two foot ore streak for twenty feet. At about midway of the adit an incline drift has been run to the southeast showing the vein clearly defined and in ore. A shaft is also down on the property to a depth of twenty odd feet. Out of this there has been a quantity of good ore taken and sacked, it being found in bunches connected with each other by thin ore streaks. The ore of the Illinois mine is of a uniformly good grade, and will average throughout the workings about $100 per ton. The silver is found as a chloride, sulphide, and in the native state. Considerable of the ore carrys a fair percentage of lead, sufficiently so to make it desirable for that metal, was there a local market for it.

The south extension of the Illinois is owned by Harris and Perkins. It has a ten foot shaft and shows ore that assays low in silver.

The Good Will lies southeast of the Illinois, and is owned by Roach, Ferguson and Dawson. It is opened by a fifteen foot shaft, and has a fair streak of ore. Assays show a value of $30.00.

The U. S. claim lies west of the Illinois and is developed by a seventy-five foot shaft. It shows fine indications of mineral in the bottom and promises to reach ore, which in character will be like that of the Bullion and Superior.

The Gray Horse, owned by Dugan, McNally and Donohoe, has

a shaft sixty feet deep with several minor surface openings. It shows ore in all the openings made, and these are seemingly along the line of a fracture in the surface limestone, which from appearances and the nature of the ore held by them, would seem to indicate the presence of an interstratified ore deposit at greater depth. The assays of this ore have been of a very flattering kind, the average being upwards of $100.

The Southwest, owned by Frazer and Holt, is located about two miles south from Kingston, and under development made this spring is proving to be a mine of excellent merit. It is opened by a shaft sunk upon a large body of ore, which carries silver in good quantities. It is located upon a contact-fissure vein.

The Big Thing, owned by Chase & Co., is located upon the summit of Kentuck mountain. It has been worked actively for several months by a force of five men, and shows eight feet of ore that runs $40 in silver. It is a claim of exceeding good promise.

The Seaside is situated upon one of the hills northeast of Kingston and has a streak of ore varying from twelve to twenty inches, from which some very high assay returns have been obtained. It is owned by Dansby, Bryson and others.

Besides those mentioned in more or less detail in the foregoing, there is a host of claims within the limits of the Middle Percha whose merits are such as to entitle them to favorable mention did the limit of this pamphlet permit of it. The east slope of Kentuck mountain and the slopes of the hills northeast and southwest of Kingston contain many such. Those of Kentuck mountain are particularly deserving and embrace the following well and favorably known properties: The Whale, Tip Top and Good Hope. Among the others are the Hilty Fraction, John S. Phelps, Sun Set, Lucky Cuss, Sun Rise, Shorty, Little Anna, Lizzie, Silver, No. 2, Van Wert, White Elephant and the Sand Flat. None of these but what have had considerable work done on them, and all show ore in more or less quantity.

In Sawpit gulch is the Yellow Jacket, showing a large vein of white quartz, with chloride stains. North of this is the Monona, located along the line of a contact-fissure, and looking well. The Condor, in the immediate vicinity, is also a good promising claim.

Immediately west of town are several good prospects. Among

them are the Humbug, Mount Auburn, Tiger and Pinon. These have veins and a mineral showing.

A group of seven claims lie just at the western edge of Kingston that are the property of Burke and Skipp. They all show defined veins and mineral. The principal ones are the Homestake, Rising Sun and Enterprise.

The Todos Santos is south of town. It has been opened in several places, and shows a crevice with favorable indications.

NORTH PERCHA.

Although identical in formation with the Middle Percha, North Percha's mines thus far are those which belong to the quartz ledge variety, described elsewhere in this pamphlet. The amount of development upon the North Percha mines is far less than is found upon the middle stream properties. A sufficient amount, however, has been done to demonstrate that there are a number of very valuable mines already there, and to show conclusively that there are many others destined to achieve notoriety in the role of ore producers.

The Solitaire mine, or as it was originally known, the Blacky, is at the head of North Percha properties. There are few who keep track of the mineral development of the west but have heard the stories of its wonderfully rich silver float, and of the subsequent sale of the property to Senator Tabor, the bonanza king of Colorado. The Solitaire is located along the course of a quartz ledge which runs in a general direction a little to the east of north and west of south. At the point where it is covered by the Solitaire location, the course is about north and south. The quartz of the ledge within the boundaries of the claim is heavily charged with silver sulphide, chloride and bromide of silver. Originally the ledge appeared upon the surface to a much greater extent than now, but the glacial action responsible for the creation of the gulch which lies west of the openings on the vein, broke it over, and the consequence is that south of the crest of the hill upon which the mine is located the ledge is apparently broken off and lost. The ledge continues to the north, running out of the lime and into and through a large porphyry dyke, but "pinching" close up in its passage through it. In fact so tight is this "pinch" that it is only traceable in many places by close observation of the pieces of porphyry float rock, bearing evidences of chemical action left by the mineral currents in their flowing. Where the ledge was broken off, as described in the foregoing, there happened to be a rich ore shoot and the consequence was that the sides of the hill were covered with immense pieces of "float" after the glacier had done its work of erosion. In the course of the ages that have since passed most of this original "float" being exposed to the corroding influences of air and water, gradually disintegrated, the quartz and other gangue matter being eaten and washed away, leaving the metal in the form of the huge chunks of sulphide of silver afterwards discovered by the prospectors. The ledge itself at the surface was also acted upon by the same natural and powerful influences, and at places along the ore shoot the silver is almost as plentiful as in the "float" which strewed the . hillside. As might be expected, however, this zone of atmospheric decomposition does not extend to any great depth upon the ledge and need hardly be looked for in the deep workings of the mine. There the ore will be found as "live rock" and while undoubtedly it will be of exceeding richness, no sensible mining man would look for it to be found as it was first discovered upon the surface. From this it will be seen and understood that the Solitaire differs only locally from the balance of the mines located upon the quartz ledges of the country. It happens to possess a richer ore shoot than any ledge yet discovered, although there is no reason to suppose but what others equally as good may be opened up. Therein lies the opportunity of the capitalist. As determined by work done, the Solitaire mine shows a shoot of ore about 500 feet in length that will average fully twenty feet wide. It dips off to the west from the surface at an angle of perhaps eighty degrees. It is opened in several places, all of which show ore in large bodies. The richest is that which lies against the east wall. The mine is now being actively developed by Mr. J. F. Tabor in the interest of his brother, Senator Tabor. Ore is being daily extracted and sacked for shipment to the market at Denver, Colorado. It is the intention of Senator Tabor to thoroughly open the mine and determine what is necessary to the successful and economical treatment of its ore. When that is decided, the proper kind of works will at once be erected and the ore handled here in the district. As now being produced, the first-class ore runs close to $1,000 per ton, while the general average of all that is taken out will exceed $300. Extensive improvements are in contemplation at this property. The price paid in all to the claimants of the mine amounted to $110,000, which included also the Saint Clair, a partial extension of the Solitaire.

The Saint Clair is located north of the Solitaire and shows croppings of the same ledge. It is also the property of Senator Tabor, having been included in the purchase of the Solitaire. The work done upon it is confined to a few surface openings of no particular consequence. Quite a considerable quantity of very rich "float" was found upon the surface of this claim at the time of its discovery.

The Brilliant lies parallel with the Solitaire and immediately west. It is owned by Jeff Raynolds, of Las Vegas, by whom it was purchased during the fall of 1882. A great deal of rich float has been taken from the surface ground of the Brilliant. This has all been assorted and sacked and is now held at the mine ready for shipment at any time. A shaft has been sunk to a depth of eighty feet and a cross-cut tunnel has been pushed in for the purpose of striking the ledge. Besides this there have been several surface openings made. In many places the Brilliant ground is covered with huge pieces of quartz carrying silver. It is undoubtedly a good piece of mining property and once it is intelligently developed will prove equal to its name.

The Silver Nugget is a fractional claim lying east of the Solitaire and between it and the Morning Star. A great deal of rich silver float was taken from the surface of this, but no work has been done upon it.

The Morning Star is owned by the Moore Bros. and McDougall. It is located east of the Solitaire in a northerly and southerly direction. Some excellent quartz has been found upon this property and high assay returns have been received from pieces subjected to test. The proximity alone of the Morning Star to the Solitaire, makes the former a valuable property.

The Nevada mine is an east and west location, its south end joining the east side of the Solitaire at the northern part of the latter property. It was located by the Moore Bros. and McDougall. It is now owned principally by a Chicago company. There is a shaft upon the property down to a depth of over seventy feet, and another surface opening in the gulch at the south end of the claim. This latter shows quartz. The shaft is all in iron stained porphyry.

The Oxford, owned by the Moore Bros. and McDougall, is located south of the Brilliant and shows a well defined ledge of quartz that contains silver in very appreciable quantities. Quite an amount of work has been done upon it, consisting of two shafts and three drifts. The ledge is seventeen feet wide where exposed on the surface and the assay values range from thirty-two to forty-two ounces.

The Bodie joins the Solitaire at the south end line of the latter and has a good ledge of quartz. Only a small amount of development has been done on it, but enough is shown to demonstrate that it possesses considerable prospective merit.

The Hillsboro mine lies northeast of the Solitaire about a mile, and is a property which has already attracted much attention because of the good width of the mineral bearing ledge it shows, and also on account of the high average value of the ore produced by it. It is owned by the Black Range Mining Company, a San Francisco corporation, with a capital stock of $10,000,000. In the upper workings, the quartz produced has an unusually high average, carrying chloride, bromide and ruby silver, quite profusely. The high grade quartz is fully four feet in width, and is traceable for a long distance upon the surface. The Hillsboro is one of the mines which the Percha district looks forward to to sustain the reputation it now possesses as a rich mining district, and in this the Hillsboro will not be disappointing. Morris Hoeflich, the well known California and Comstock mining man is at the head of the company owning this property.

The Chapeau, joining the Hillsboro, is owned by F. J. Wilson and M. W. Wallace. It shows a vein in limestone that varies in width from two to eight feet so far as opened. There has been a total of 110 feet of work done upon it. At a point 200 feet above the lower workings, there is a defined contact of lime and porphyry, showing a heavy blossom of black iron and manganese. The vein worked upon is apparently a spur leading to the contact, and carries a gangue composed of quartz, spar and talc. Assays from the claim have returned from $250 to $4,000.

The Harkaway is owned by Carnahan and Barr. It has two

different veins crossing it. There is a ten-foot assessment shaft and a number of surface openings.

The Silver is owned by Carnahan and Barr. It is developed by a shaft down twenty-five feet on a contact vein, following the foot wall. There is a ten-inch showing of black talc, mineralized. The vein is three feet wide and almost perpendicular. Some fine specimens of ore have been produced from this property, showing chloride and native silver.

The Bullion and Belle of Percha make favorable showings, the latter in particular having an immense outcropping of quartz.

The Percha Chief is owned by J. W. McCuistion, Ed. Kelley and A. J. Shaw. The shaft shows an iron capping nearly vertical, changing into quartz at a depth of nine feet. The vein is well defined and easily traced.

The Osceola, is owned by A. J. Shaw and F. M. Meyers. It has a twelve-foot vertical shaft, and an incline shaft twenty feet deep. Good ore has been produced from both of these openings. A large cropping of quartz upon this claim shows some rich ore.

The Gamewell is owned by McCuistion, Kelley and Shaw. It is located on the same vein as the Osceola. It has a shaft twelve feet deep.

The Comet is owned by Blaine and McLaughlin. It is a fissure in porphyry, carrying a quartz gangue bearing silver sulphurets. It is opened by an adit level on the vein to a distance of forty-five feet. This level leaves the ore to the right most of the way, but it is ready to take out any time.

The Temperate Zone and Comet lie parallel with each other and are owned by W. H. Hume and others. The vein of the Temperate Zone is of good width and has yielded some very fine ore.

The Gem is owned by Fitzpatrick, Shannon and Fox. Shows a vein from ten to twelve feet in width and are now in on it twenty-two feet. Several good assay returns have been obtained from the Gem, one going $260 in silver. The average returns are from $60 to $70.

The Homestake joins the Gem on the southwest, and is located upon the same vein. No work of consequence is done. It is owned by Fitzpatrick, Shannon and Fox. Assays run from $5.00 to $100.

The Eclipse shows two veins carrying considerable iron, and has produced ore running from $25 to $40. About twenty-five feet of work has been done upon it consisting of shafts and open cuts. It is owned by Fitzpatrick, Shannon and Fox.

The Pennsylvania is owned by D. S. Foster, Chas. Bishop, Thos. Fay and Dr. B. G. Guthrie. It is a large, well defined lode, showing sulphurets of iron, carrying silver. An open-cut is excavated upon the vein six to eight feet in length.

The Utah is owned by Burke, Skipp and Richie. It shows a fine, large quartz ledge which has been sunk upon to a depth of forty feet. Ore from this shaft assays very well.

The Wild Deer is owned by Moore Bros. and McDougall. It has a large quartz ledge, fifteen feet in width, and is opened by a fifteen-foot shaft.

The Maud Muller lies west of the Saint Clair and is owned by Jeff Raynolds. A great deal of very rich "float" has been taken from the surface of this claim, but as yet no ore has been discovered in place. Several surface openings have been made upon the property.

The Keystone is a very promising quartz ledge. It is located west from the Solitaire and shows ore at the outcrop similar in appearance to that produced by the Solitaire. Assays run very high. It it owned by Darst, Nickle and others, and is being developed steadily.

The Mountain View is owned by Burke, Skipp and Elliott. It has a fine quartz ledge. No work of consequence has yet been done, but ore off the out-crop assays $46.00.

The Glen Cove has a quartz lead, and is supplied with an excellent mill site. No work or assays.

The Silver King is owned by Mason and Overhultz. It is a quartz lead having a fifty-foot shaft upon it. Assays vary from forty to seventy-five ounces.

The Lillie D. has a quartz vein in limestone, varying from three to five feet in width. It carries ore that will run from $200 to $1,000. It is owned by Mason and Overhultz.

The Daisy Deane is owned by Shaw and Martin and has a vein carrying silver sulphurets. It is opened by an adit fifteen feet in length.

Above the town of Percha, and on the south fork of the North

Percha are the Cimarron, Grizzly, Sarah Bernhardt, Hopeful, Temperance, Pocahontas and Little Chief, all having assessment work only done upon them. They are the property of Blain, Bentley and others.

Besides those mentioned there are in other portions of the Percha district a great number of claims the names of which it was impossible to secure. Some of them are equal to many of those which have been written of in the preceding pages. Among them are the Fay, Butler, Golden Crown, Silver Tip, Illinois, Lillie Gamewell, Grey Eagle, Sweet Ann, Casandra, Revenue, Golconda, North Texan, Valdemar, Alpha, Jackass and Sam Tilden.

Up the gulch, east of Percha City, are the Sooner, H. Seeley. Burke, Corry, Gorringe and Gorringe extension.

About three miles up the North Percha there is a class of mines which are referred to in the description of the formation given in this pamphlet, as fissures in trachyte. Of late these have begun to receive attention at the hands of prospectors, and a more intimate knowledge of the indications presented by them at the outcrops is being taken advantage of. The result is seen in the new strikes that are being heard of as occurring in the section noted. They present no surface ore for inspection, the only indication being a quartz cropping, carrying iron sulphurets, and usually barren of metallic values at the apex of the veins. As developed thus far, the iron gives place to other compounds, and the ore makes its appearance as a base mass of quartz carrying chloride, sulphide and ruby silver, associated with other and baser metals, such as zinc, arsenic and antimony. The grade of the ore, however, is high enough to neutralize the ill effect that such a combination usually has upon ores of only ordinary value. In many mining countries veins occurring in trachyte or porphyritic rocks are regarded as likely to be of comparatively shallow depth. When these rocks form the overlie of a mining country such is apt to be the case, but when, as in the Percha district, they are intrusive and have not overflowed, and constitute the formation of a large section, veins found in them may be relied upon to continue to the lowest workable depths, and far below. Only one example of them is yet to be seen, as but one has been opened sufficiently to allow of a partial determination of its prospective merits.

The Keystone is the mine referred to in the last sentence of the preceding paragraph. It is owned by Thomas and Purple. It is a vertical vein in **trachyte**. There **is an** adit level run **in on** the vein for a **distance** of about fifty **feet**. Where this **level was** started the vein **was** about one foot and a half wide. The iron **was** passed through **at about** sixteen feet, the vein widening at that point to three **and a** half feet, and good ore coming in. At thirty feet an**other** change occurred, brittle and ruby making its appearance, the **ore** also showing zinc blende. The hanging wall has been followed **and** now at the **breast of the** level there are three **and a** half feet of ore. Of this **about fourteen inches** is exceedingly rich and **will** average not less than **$500 per ton,** the balance is ore that will **mill** anywhere from $50 to $75. Only the **hanging** wall is **shown at the** face of the level, the vein having widened **out** so that the balance is all mineral bearing crevice matter. A **great deal** of ore has been extracted from this mine and **a** shipment **of** several tons will have been made by the **time** this pamphlet makes its appearance.

Extensions **of the** Keystone are located for quite a distance, upon the same vein, and the fact **that** the vein is so clearly defined and crops so prominently for so long a distance, argues much in favor of its merits as a source from which large amounts of ore may **yet** be taken. Some of these extensions are being developed rapidly and the same general characteristics are apparent so far as work **has** been done, as were to be seen upon the Keystone itself—at the same stage. Local mine operators **have this** spring entered into contract to develop some **of** the extensions of the Keystone and claims located upon similar veins in the neighborhood **are now being** looked after by the shrewd mining men of this section.

SOUTH PERCHA.

Although showing surface indications and formative peculiarities similar in all respects to those of the Middle and North Percha, the South Percha has **not yet** been proved up to even such a limited extent as is true of the **others**. The leading property of the district has been tied **up in** litigation for some time and to this as much as anything else is due, perhaps, the inactivity which has prevailed.

The Grey Eagle **is** owned by John S. Stacy, J. J. Avey, L. R. Routh **and** G. A. Cassil. It is a mine which illustrates in a remarkable manner **one of** the peculiarities **of** the vein phenomena of the

Percha district, and at the same time opens the eyes of the investigator to another new and extremely interesting field of mineral research. This, because so far as yet known it is entirely unlike any other mine yet discovered hereabouts, and is representative of a class of mines that may yet prove important factors in the make-up of those upon which the town of Kingston depends for support. Those who have read the description of the formation as given in the preceding pages of this pamphlet, will remember it is stated that "In some places the porphyry fails to intrude itself clear through the limestone to the surface, but after rising to a certain plane, has spread out and is found in the condition of an interstratafication in the sedimentary rocks. Hence it is that the lime sometimes appears overlying the porphyry." The formation of the Grey Eagle vein is a perfect illustration of this. The ore is found lying on top of the porphyry and underneath the limestone, which latter rock forms the surface of the hill into which the main workings have been driven. The consequence is that so far as exposed the vein is a contact, with a lime hanging and a porphyry, or trachyte foot wall. As it was originally formed the vein would never have been discovered, but the erosive force that made the Lake fork of South Percha canon, scored off the mass of overlying rock down to and below the apex of the vein, at the particular point where the prospectors discovered it. This erosion also caused the apex of the vein to assume a horseshoe course so that now it is traceable from a point where it rises out of the bed of the creek at the east, westerly about 800 feet, southerly across the creek and then easterly back again for a long distance, conforming always to the contour of the hills through which it passes. The vein shows continuously for a distance of several thousand feet, and varies in width at the different openings, from two to fifteen feet. It is exposed in numerous workings, the principal being those on the Grey Eagle mine. The first is a small cut just above the creek, which shows approach to the vein and will probably reach it in a few feet further. The second is an adit in about fifteen feet showing a splendid breast of ore. The third is farther up the hill upon the course of the vein and has also an excellent showing of ore in sight. On the south bank of the creek a tunnel is in about twenty-five feet but evidently below the vein, although some ore has been taken from it. Throughout the excavations the ore is continuous and is a strongly defined shoot, the chief portion of it appearing to be upon the north side of the creek and pitching a little to the east of north. The ore is a mixture of lead carbonate, antimonial galena, green and blue carbonate of copper, with some arsenic and sulphide of zinc. It is an exceedingly attractive ore to the eye as may be imagined, and specimens of great beauty are frequently obtained. With development the **ore** might naturally be looked **for** to change **and assume a** standard **of** character different in some respects from that now found, but retaining essentially the predominant characteristics which now mark it. The gangue or matrix of the ore is quartz, and where the lead carbonate is found its origin is due to the desulphurization of what was originally galena, hence the honeycombed appearance of that class of the surface ore seen at this mine. Although somewhat refractory in its composition the ore of the Grey Eagle is of a grade sufficiently valuable to make **the** operation of the mine a work of profit when home smelters commence operations. The change that will undoubtedly follow upon development may also have a bearing for the better upon the grade of the ore. Undoubtedly this property is one of great value at present and its future, owing to the peculiarities of its occurrence, is pregnant with vast possibilities. The assays from the ore indicate a value running from $16 to $80 and up as high as $500 in silver per ton, from twenty to forty per cent. in lead and from ten to twenty per cent. in copper. Six ounces in gold was also obtained from one assay. Its title is at present unsettled owing to a dispute regarding **the** rightful ownership. Lockwood Mead and William Mead claim the property by right of priority of discovery under the name of the Bismarck mine. Pending the settlement of **the** suit to decide the question **of** ownership, no work is being done upon the property. This will come **up** at the fall term of the court, at Silver City, and it is to be hoped will be decided at that time. So highly promising a property should not be allowed to lie dormant, when it might be made largely and profitably productive.

The American Eagle, Humming Bird, Black Eagle, Little Michigan, Lone Star, Enterprise and Monitor claims surround the Grey Eagle and cover the apex of **the vein** when it passes out of the boundary lines of that claim. All **of** these have been worked upon and while there is **no** such showing **as is** to be found in the

Grey Eagle yet there are many things which point to a future value for these claims that will not be inconsiderable. The American Eagle is owned by Marcus Fuller and A. B. Stacy; the Morning Star, Little Michigan and Enterprise, by H. H. Barton, James Barnes and G. A. Cassil. The Black Eagle is under the same ownership as the Grey Eagle. All of these claims are covered with a fine growth of timber, and are well situated for convenient and economical working.

The Southwest mine, owned by Frazer and Holt, is located along the line of a contact-fissure, crossing the ridge upon the north side of South Percha creek. It shows a very pronounced blossom of oxidized iron and manganese in several places along the course of the vein. From one of these places the discoverers took ore that returned good assay results in silver but until this spring nothing but assessment work was done upon it. It has been taken under bond by a Chicago company and they have put down the shaft through the iron cap and into a large body of excellent ore, resembling in all respects that produced by the Bullion, Superior and other contact-fissure mines of this district. The value of the ore is known only to those directly interested, but it certainly is of a good grade. It has a general apparent trend towards the contact which shows west of the shaft, and will doubtless make in that direction. No better illustration than the Southwest can be cited of the chances there are for good investment in prospects here. The claims showing the iron cap upon the surface are numerous and interests in them can be obtained at very liberal terms.

The R. Lee lies north of the Grey Eagle and is owned by McArdle, Askew and Peter Johnson. The vein shows galena ore and has a twenty-foot shaft upon it.

The Black Hawk group of mines is owned by Routh and Sidney. They are situated upon the north and south slopes of the ridge lying immediately north of South Percha gulch and are located upon mineral bearing quartz ledges. The principal mine of the group is the Black Hawk. It has a north and south course and where opened shows a strong mineral impregnation. The surface quartz is heavily charged with oxidized iron and some manganese, and shows a fair assay value, that with depth may be looked for to increase. The ledge is an immense one in width and length, being one hundred feet wide in places and traceable for a long distance. Only a small amount of development work has been done upon the Black Hawk, but it will be actively operated this season. Assays from this claim show very well. The Little Jim is opened upon a contact showing quartz with a porphyry foot wall. It too will be developed this season. The Little Jim's sister adjoins and shows favorably. The Red Buffalo and Silver Hawk are the claims of the group next in importance to those mentioned and show wide ledges of quartz, carrying silver. The former is thirty feet wide in places.

The Little Nell is located upon a contact, having ore out in the lime as yet. It is of a lead character, and exists in the form of galena.

In the park at the head of the Lake fork of the South Percha there are a number of claims showing mineral indications at the surface equal in many respects to some of greater note elsewhere. One of these is the Black Signal, owned by Avey, Stacy and Fuller. There is a heavy outcrop of iron, continuing to a depth of thirty feet and how far below is not known, it having been sunk upon that deep. The Iron Chief is of the same character and showing, and is owned by the same parties. A quartz ledge at one end shows copper and iron pyrites.

McArdle and Askew own a claim in the park that shows a contact carrying a large body of iron and some quartz.

A prominent, and in some respects a remarkable feature of the South Percha, is what is locally termed the "big iron ledge." by the prospectors of the district. It extends around the hills on either side of the gulch, and circumscribes an area of considerable extent. This area is entirely made up of porphyry with quartz ledges cutting through it, while outside is the lime. The peculiar shape, it being oviform, is due to the erosion which made the South Percha gulch and its tributary streams. Along the course of this ledge and following its windings, are located a large number of claims, many of which show upon development extremely good indications for mines yet to be discovered. The outcrop is iron throughout, but this has in no instance been entirely sunk through. Many of the claims produce ore assaying quite well. The following list comprises the principal prospects located upon it:

The Black Diamond has assessment work done upon it and

shows a large body of oxidized iron. It is owned by Walsh and Breen.

The Elk, owned by Ed. Baird and Wm. Mead, shows oxidized iron and has assessment work done on it.

The Mint, owned by Foran, White, Evans and Richie, has a forty-foot shaft, all in iron, assaying from $12 to $20.

The Belcher is owned by Lester Dumm. It is opened by a twenty-foot adit, all in oxidized iron. High assays are reported from this claim.

The Overland, owned by Frank Foran and Del White, is perhaps the claim having the most openings and showing the best results. There is a shaft down forty feet and several minor openings, all showing very favorably. The deep shaft was sunk at a point where at a shallow depth the iron was passed through and a vein of ore carrying lead as galena and carbonate was encountered. Assays from average samples of this ore returned $20 in silver and 54 per cent. lead. There are several feet of this ore in the vein. Important discoveries may be looked for as more work is done upon the Overland.

The Golden Circle is owned by Richie and Evans. It is down ten feet with a large body of oxidized iron.

The Garfield is owned by Petit and Dumm. It has a forty-foot shaft in iron, and high assays are reported from it.

The Mountain Girl is owned by Petit and Dumm, and has a showing like the others described. Assessment work done.

The Golden Gate is owned by Foran, White and Blunn. An assessment shaft shows a large body of iron.

The Wild Turkey, owned by Baird and Hardy, has assessment work done upon it, with a large iron showing.

The Leadville is owned by Ed. Baird. No work on it yet, but a big surface out-crop of iron.

The Yellow Jacket is owned by Foran and White and has assessment work done upon it.

The Richmond is owned by Phillips, Bevan, Carey and Stover. It is developed by three cross-cut tunnels. As yet none of these has encountered the hanging wall and all are in vein stuff composed chiefly of oxidized iron. The main tunnel is in eighty feet, the next forty feet and the third thirty feet. Out of one of these tunnels ore has been taken which assayed 260 ounces in silver.

The Charlie Richie is owned by Richie and Evans. It has a large surface showing but no work is done yet.

The foregoing embraces as stated the principal prospects upon the "big iron ledge." They are owned mostly by poor men, unable to do the work necessary to prove them up to the point of profitableness. Parties so disposed can obtain good bargains upon the whole or a part of most of them, either in cash purchases or in interests for for a stated amount of work. The "iron cap" which is so extensive is usually regarded as one of the best possible indications in a mining country, and deep development has proven it to be so in the mines of the Percha district. Wherever sunk through ore has been found. The indigent prospector, or claim owner, however, has the will but not the means to do the necessary work, as it takes money to buy "grub and tools," and he is proverbially short of both. It is an especially inviting field for the capitalist or others with money to invest. The conditions favorable to the making of mines are there, but the ability to do this is lacking upon the part of the owners.

Foran, Baird and White have four claims down the creek that are showing up well under the development that has been done upon them. They are the Ontario, Calleo, Stonewall and Clipper. The Ontario is the leading claim, and has a quartz ledge heavily charged with iron. Five shafts have been sunk upon it, the principal ones having attained depths of seventy, fifty-five and thirty-five feet respectively. The other two are of shallower depth. In each of these shafts the showing was practically the same, and out of them ore has been taken that has returned by assay $25, $65 and $110 per ton.

The Sunset claim is owned by McManus, Askew and McArdle. It has a quartz ledge showing ore that according to an assay test carries $34 in silver.

A short distance above the saw mill there is a large spar ledge upon which a number of claims are located, but without ore results as yet.

In additon to the foregoing there are numerous other claims scattered throughout the South Percha, possessing considerable merit as properties of prospective value, and to which the same general remarks given in the foregoing will also apply. Among them are the Little Chief, Iron Mountain, Enterprise, Knobel, Oro Cash. Horseshoe, McMicken, Mountain Boy, Lucky Cuss, Mountain Peak and Tammany. There are, as intimated, others, but it would be a work of impossibility almost to attempt to collate the individual claims that have been located, and the task has not been tried. Enough, however, has been shown to demonstrate the object of this pamphlet, viz: to call attention to the indisputable fact that the various sections of the Percha district are ripe for the investment of capital and the results following such investment will surely be of a kind that will greatly redound to the credit not only of the whole of the country surrounding the town of Kingston, but of the Territory of New Mexico besides.

TRIBUTARY DISTRICTS.

Although the Middle, North and South Percha gulches properly constitute what is known as the Percha mining district, yet there are several sections which have assumed leading places as possessing mines of merit, and whose business through natural causes is attracted towards the center of the Percha country—Kingston. Prominent among these is

TRUJILLO CREEK.

The mines at and near the head of this stream have for some months past been attracting considerable attention, and as much prospecting has been done there as is true perhaps of any other locality outside of the Perchas themselves.

The Monaska company's claims constitute the leading property of the locality, and comprise the Traitor, Monaska and 7-20. The members of the company are F. E. Everett, A. L. Jones, John McLaughlin, E. W. Bush and J. Frick. E. W. Bush was the discoverer and locator of the claims. The Traitor and Monaska both have some work done upon them, but the "strike" was made and the workings are chiefly confined to the 7-20. The vein is a vertical fissure in limestone, carrying a gangue of lime spar and quartz. The ore cropped out on the surface in an eighteen-inch streak and has held out continuously as depth upon it has been attained. The main shaft is down 140 feet, following ore from the surface, and has made a handsome production that possesses a very high average value in silver. During the latter part of the month of April last several tons were assorted and shipped to Denver, Colo. This **ore** gave very high returns in silver. A sample sack of the lot averaged at the rate of over $800 per ton. The ore out and remaining on the dump will average upwards of $100 per ton. At the bottom of the shaft the pay vein is about twenty-four inches in width, with every indication of widening, and shows ore all of which is equal and most of it superior to the average of that already produced. In the bottom of an open-cut along the vein there is also a well-defined streak of ore eighteen inches wide. The silver is in the form of sulphide, with occasional pieces of native. The owners of this property are able and experienced mining men and will work it to the end that a large and steady product may be made.

Fitzpatrick and Parker are developing a claim near by the Monaska company's property. It is a spar ledge, in appearance and character like that of the 7-20 mine. No ore has yet been produced from it.

The Bald Eagle, Buckstone and Maud S. are claims in the vicinity upon which some work has been done with fair results. They are the property of Parke and others. The Buckstone has a shaft seventy feet deep and has produced some excellent crevice matter. The Bald Eagle is sunk upon to a depth of forty-five feet, showing crevice matter. The Maud S. has been penetrated twenty feet with excellent results. At a depth of six feet it produced mineral-bearing matter that assayed $69.80, and although no other assays have been made since, the same stuff is still in the bottom.

The Consolidated, owned by Webber, Bealert and Fowler, is showing up quite nicely. A shaft down twenty feet has produced some very excellent ore.

Farther to the east than the claims just mentioned, and situated at the head of Trujillo creek, are a number of prospects which are quite noted for strength of vein and presence of ore. They are upon what might be termed the extension of the Grey Eagle mine, and joins the South Percha extensions of that property, where the ore zone upon which it is situated crosses in its course over into and through Trujillo and Tierra Blanca districts. The ore is a quartz base, carrying galena and carbonate of lead in large quantities. A great deal of work has been done upon these claims and in many instances the showing is sufficient to warrant the belief that mines of splendid productive capabilities will yet result upon further development. The limits of this pamphlet are insufficient to properly describe the individual merits of these properties. Almost without exception they show ore of a very desirable lead character, carrying silver enough upon an average to make the work of operating **them** one of profit, when undertaken with a determination to properly develop before expecting large returns. Immense pieces of lead "float" and ore from the veins are exhibited at Kingston, which cannot fail to convince one of the great future that is in store for the mines producing them.

Barnaby, Parker and Watson are the owners of the Mountain Boy, Hunter, Lucy D., Captain B., Whipoorwill, Lookout and Omega. Of these, the Captain B., Lookout and Omega have the most work done upon them, and show highly favorable results in the way of ore out and in place in the vein. The Iris, Black Hawk and Keystone, **also** owned by Barnaby, Parker and Watson, are located upon **an** ore belt parallel with the one described and show quite favorably.

There is a host of other claims located north and south from those described, and apparently on the same veins. All have more or less development upon them, while none differ materially in characteristics from those as briefly described in the foregoing.

Proceeding south from Trujillo creek, across the ridges which make down from the summit of the range, the same ore veins **are** traceable for miles and only pass the confines of one gulch to enter within those of another. Thus it is, as already indicated, that the mines of the parallel gulches are in reality what might be called "extensions" of each other, being all located upon the different parallel mineral veins or ledges which course through the country from north to south.

TIERRA BLANCA.

This section is one of the oldest mining localities in the Black Range, claims having been staked off there several years ago. The leading mines are those which lie up near the head of the creek, and upon the ore belt described as cutting across from Trujillo creek.

The Seven Brothers is owned by T. E. Fitzpatrick and Captain Dawson, of the U. S. army. This is a particularly fine prospect and has had considerable work done upon it. It is opened by an incline shaft eighty **feet** deep, **in** ore continuously, **varying in** width from three to five feet. There are 100 tons on the dump that will range in value from $40 to $500 in silver and gold, and average about twenty-five per cent. in lead.

The Bob Lincoln is close by and has an eighty-foot incline shaft with a showing of ore on dump and underground.

The other prominent claims are Oliver Twist, Blue Jay, Oriole, Republican and Lee.

Hartman & Maxwell, the well known mining and real estate brokers of Kingston, have a group of fine properties, bearing galena **and** carbonate ores. **From** these specimens of great size and importance have been produced, and there **remains no** doubt but that rich and profuse disclosures of ore will be made upon development of the prospects producing them.

Situated still southward, and in the manner described, there are numerous others going on over into the Berenda creek, where some excellent prospects are to be found.

The Victoria and Silver King, are a couple of splendidly promising mines situated east of the claim mentioned in the foregoing. From them some excellent ore has been taken and everything about them presage mines of importance, when once they are opened up.

IRON CREEK.

This section lies about four and a half miles west of Kingston, upon the western slope of the Black Range, and is noted for the great strength and grade of its ore bodies. It has attracted considerable attention in the past few years and is doing so at the present time. The veins are immense and wonderfully prolific of lead ores, some of the location monuments, even, being built of galena ore. The principal operations there are now being carried on by Marshall Dansby, an old miner and prospector, in the interests of himself and a Las Vegas company. A Mexican adobe smelter is being run with good success upon ore produced from the **district. A.** Barnaby, Bradford & Troeger and Col. Parker, all of Kingston, are largely interested in the mines of Iron creek and own properties showing vast bodies of a highly desirable lead ore. The claims showing abundance of surface indications, but lacking development, are numerous, and in consequence the investor has an inviting field before him.

About eight miles north from Kingston is what is known as the "True Fissure district," a portion of the territory embraced within the limits of Cave Creek. There is a large number of very promising silver mines, that with a small amount of development show up splendidly. The Silver Wave and Trade Dollar, owned by John McCann, are parallel veins, the former averaging from four to seven feet in width, and the latter from two to three feet. The average assay results from these mines are high, running close to $100 per ton. Among other good prospects are the Mammoth, Hard Cash, Northern Belle, Quien Sabe, Polar Star, Adventurer, Lookout, Winnebago Chief, Hancock, Ingersoll and Clifford.

ADDENDA.

Since the greater portion of this pamphlet was put in type there have been many and important changes in the status of our principal mines. These changes invariably are for the better and go a great way in determining the future of the Percha district and the town of Kingston. It is a notable fact that wherever development has been carried out to any depth that increased value resulted not only in quantity but in quality of the ore bodies. The Superior mine, particularly, is showing up magnificently, the incline shaft having reached the level of the rich ore bodies first struck in the winze on the contact. The consequence is seen in the immense body of high grade ore now exposed, and from which shipments will be made steadily The Bullion mine has reached the contact and the source of its rich ore bodies in the limestone is about to be discovered. Shipments have been steady and of uniformly high grade ore. The Iron King has developed an immense deposit of sand carbonate ore, from which fifteen tons daily can be taken, the result of exploitatory work alone. Anent the the Iron King, an error is apparent in the statement of its purchase price and the locality of those comprising the company. It was bought by New York people, and $30,000 paid for three-fourths of the property, originally, the remaining fourth being afterward purchased for $15,000. New developments of much importance have also been made at the Miners' Dream, Brush Heap, Southwest and Seaside, while over at the head of the North Percha the fissures in the trachyte are the center of mining attention, some new and important ore bodies being lately revealed. The Falls mine, close to the Keystone, is showing a fine body of ore. Upon the whole, it can be said without fear of successful contradiction, that the Percha district presents a more flattering prospect for the future than is true of any other in New Mexico.

www.ingramcontent.com/pod-product-compliance
Lightning Source LLC
Chambersburg PA
CBHW031221290326
41931CB00036B/1198